PUMPKIN CIRCLE

The Story of a Garden

Story by George Levenson

Photography by Shmuel Thaler

Tricycle Press
Berkeley/Toronto

The pumpkin seed

makes the pumpkin plant, and the

pumpkin plant

makes pumpkins.

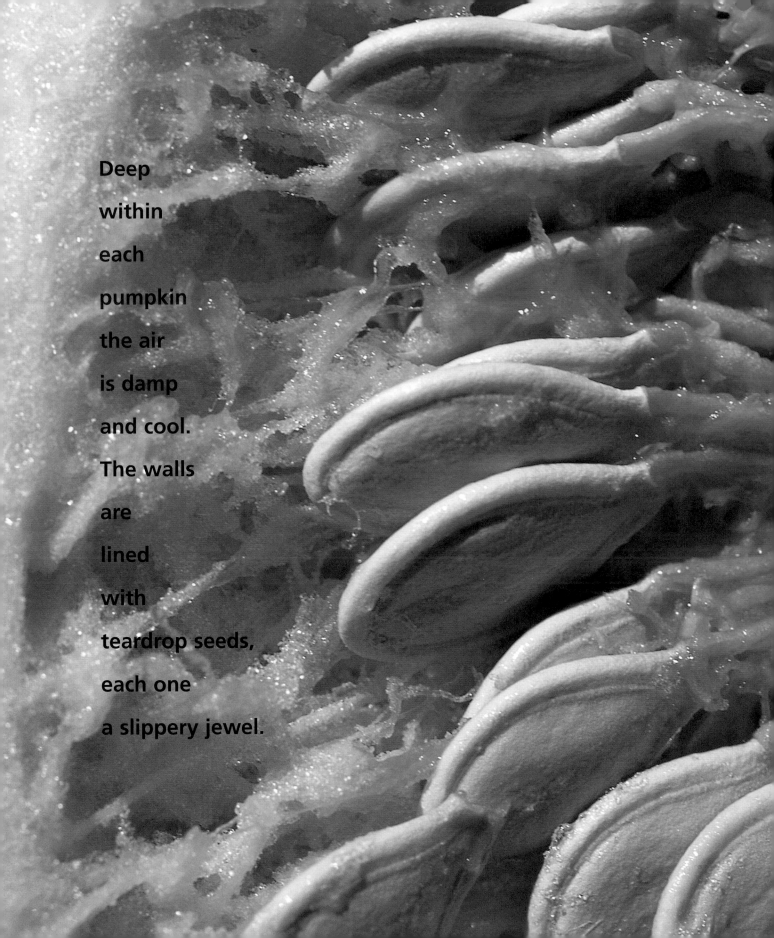

Deep

within

each

pumpkin

the air

is damp

and cool.

The walls

are

lined

with

teardrop seeds,

each one

a slippery jewel.

Scrape them from their orange cave. Wash away squishy mush.

Save a few to grow next spring, and have a bunch to munch.

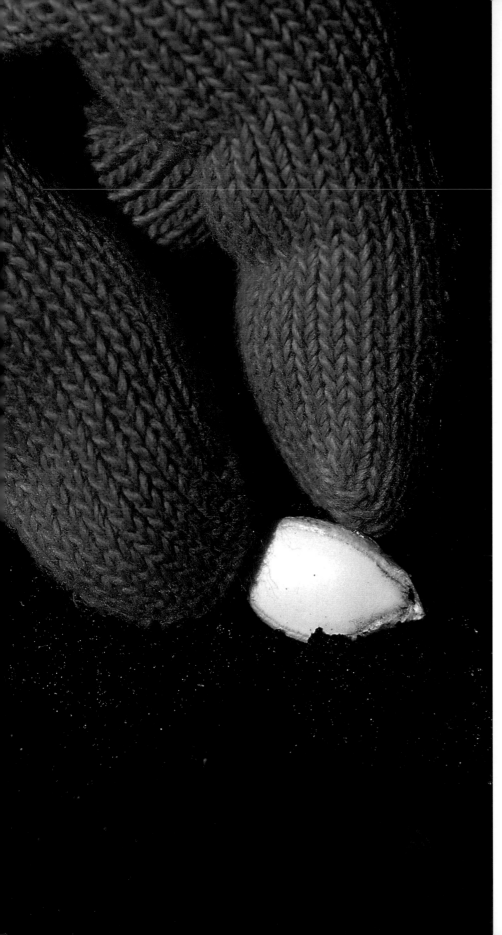

When the earth

is soft and warm,

plant

those sleeping seeds.

In about one week, out they peek,

two fresh, young, fat green leaves.

This garden will be home to many pumpkin cousins—

Spooky, Max, and Lumina,

Le Grand and tiny Munchkin

One big pumpkin family, five varieties,

each one started from

different pumpkin seeds.

Every passing minute

awakens each new plant,

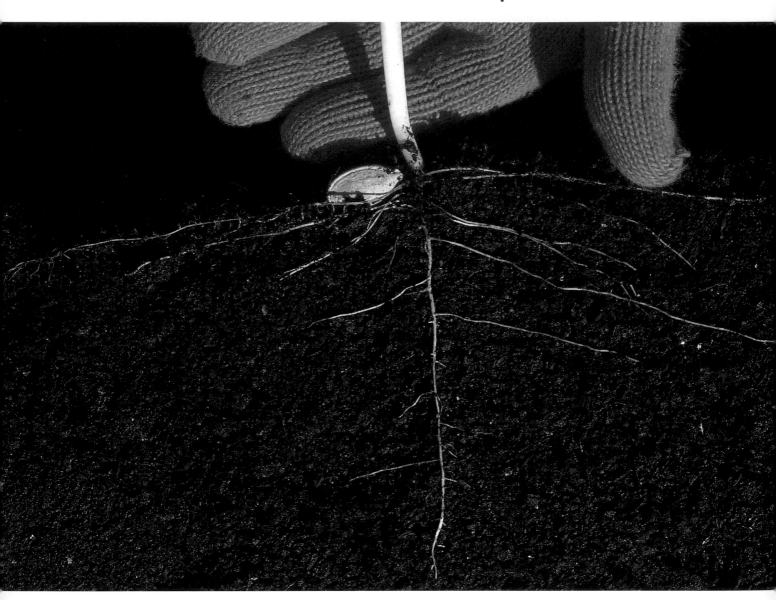

reaching down with silky roots,

reaching up to dance.

Week by week

the backyard patch

spreads before your eyes,

filling every inch of space

with leaves and roots and vines.

Huge green leaves grow toward the sky, prickly, lush, and wide.

They soak up sun and water,

and make a shady place to hide.

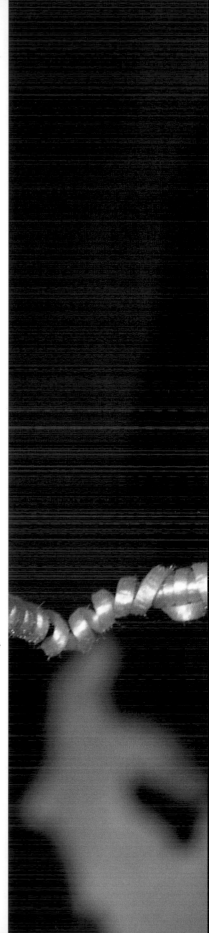

Twisty tendrils grasp like hands
stretching out to cling.

They roll down into fancy curls
and wind up just like springs.

Then, silently as angels, flower buds appear

with pointy little collars and gleaming silver hair.

Velvet petals open,

brilliant sunlit bowls,

delicately fragrant—

a sign

of

pumpkin

gold!

Along come the bees

floating through the air,

buzzing, gathering, guzzling—

zooming everywhere!

Butterflies and spiders,
grasshoppers and snails,
explore the pumpkin garden
as they travel private trails.

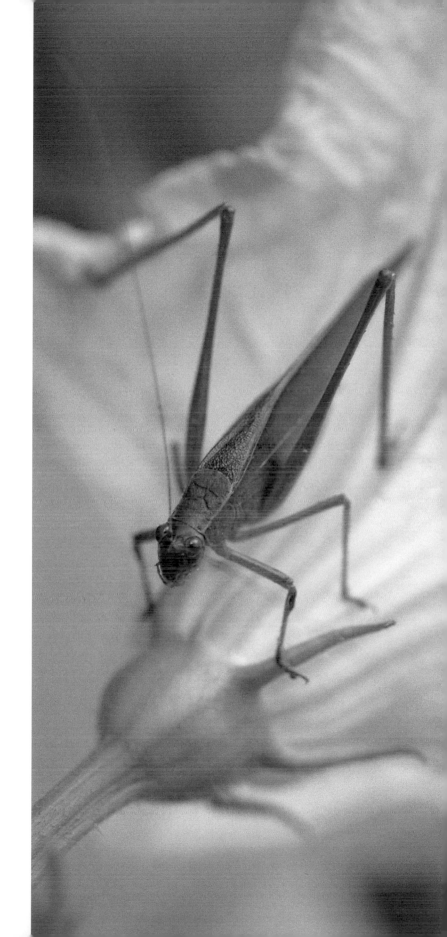

Pumpkins climbing up the fence.

Pumpkins everywhere!

Help those pumpkins sit up straight

so they grow up round and proud.

Scratch on pumpkin names

so they stand out in the crowd.

Or just sit back.

Enjoy the view.

Pumpkins grow because pumpkins know

exactly what to do.

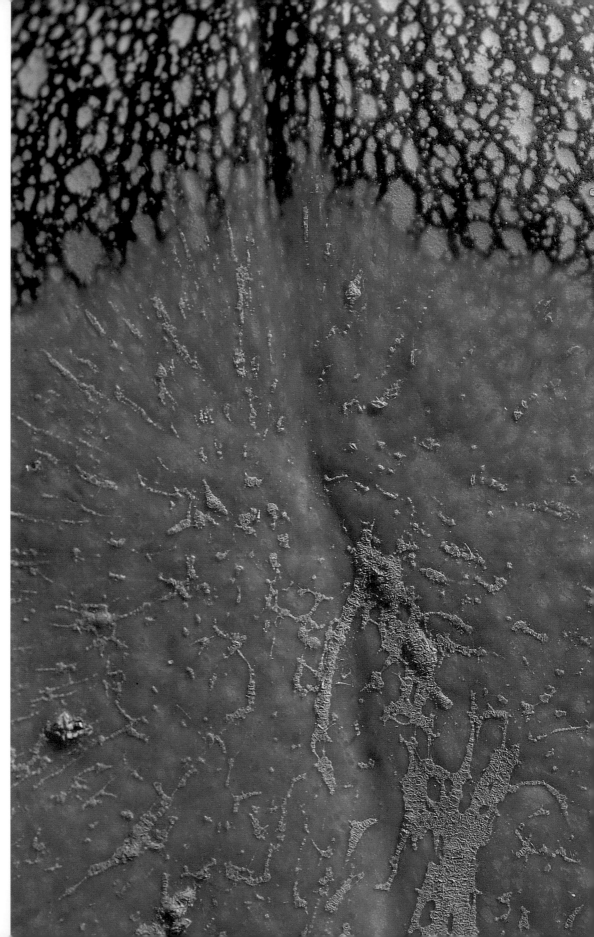

When
summer
turns
to fall

green
turns
to gold.

Shorter
days
bring
chilly
nights
and
pumpkin
vines
grow
old.

Now comes the harvest.

Pluck treasures from the vine.

Clear away lifeless leaves.

Hide the rags of time.

Gather up the finished fruit,
ripe and fully grown.
Tidy up the garden.
Make a cozy pumpkin home.

Salute the pumpkin circle!
Make way for pumpkin cheer.
Behold the pumpkin miracle.

We're pumpkin millionaires!

Make up pumpkin faces.

Add bright candlelight.

Set them on your doorstep,

let them flicker through the night.

Every day

those pumpkins change—

getting older,

getting strange.

Sinking, shrinking

pumpkin,

back to earth
you go,

turning into
muck and dirt—

a place for seeds
to grow.

How did this begin?

What is this pumpkin thing?

Is there a Mother Nature?

Is there a Pumpkin King?

We can be sure of this:

It's a circle without end.

It's pumpkin seeds

to pumpkins

to pumpkin seeds again!

How to Grow Pumpkins

Varieties

There are many varieties of pumpkin seeds, and each pumpkin is unique. Pumpkins come in colors ranging from white to orange to flaming red, and can weigh anywhere from a few ounces to over 500 pounds.

Where, When, and How to Plant

Choose a sunny spot that gets at least 6 hours of direct daily sunlight. Sow seeds in the spring when temperatures reach the low 70s. Mound rich, loosely packed soil into hills about 3 feet in diameter. Plant 4 to 5 seeds in the tops of the hills, 1 inch deep. Seedlings will sprout in 7 to 14 days. Pumpkins need about 120 growing days.

Growth and Reproduction

During the first 10 weeks, the pumpkin plant is devoted to leaf, root, and vine development. Then come the flower buds. The male flowers (page 19), which appear first, sit on long thin stems. The female flowers (page 18) grow closer to the vine and rest like queens on fuzzy round thrones—baby pumpkins in waiting. The bees are the matchmakers, gathering pollen from the male flowers and depositing it inside the female flowers while they guzzle sweet nectar.

Protection

Gophers, moles, vine borers, beetles, aphids, and powdery mildew are among the unwelcome visitors and conditions that plague the hardy pumpkin plant. Throughout the season, keep an eye out for any irregularities, especially in the leaves, and consult your garden center for remedies. A healthy well-fed plant, basking in sunlight, unburdened by competition from weeds, and properly watered, has the best chance of resisting danger and recovering from attack.

Special Effects

To encourage the classic round pumpkin, adjust the young fruit so that its bottom sits squarely on the ground. To inscribe names on pumpkins, wait until the fruit is at least the size of a tennis ball. Using a nail, scratch letters onto the pumpkin. Be careful not to penetrate the skin more than $1/8$ inch deep, and immediately wipe the markings. The letters will seal over and expand as the pumpkin grows bigger.

Harvest Tips

When clipping pumpkins from the vine, leave several inches of stem—this helps them stay fresh longer. Store the pumpkins in a dry cool place, and they might last until spring.

For more details, consult the Pumpkin Circle Website at http://www.pumpkincircle.com.

Text copyright © 1999 by George Levenson
Photographs on pages 1 (seed background), 4, 11, 15, 19, 23, 24, 25, 30, 36, 37, and 40 (signs and bottom image) © 1999 by George Levenson
All other photographs © 1999 by Shmuel Thaler

Tricycle Press
an imprint of Ten Speed Press
P.O. Box 7123
Berkeley, California 94707
www.tricyclepress.com

Interior design by George Levenson and Tasha Hall
Cover design by Jean Sanchirico
Type set in Frutiger
Developmental editing by Barbara Fuller

Library of Congress Cataloging-in-Publication Data

Levenson, George.
Pumpkin circle / George Levenson; photographs by Shmuel Thaler.
  p. cm.
Summary: Rhyming text and photographs follow a pumpkin patch as it grows and changes, from seeds to plants to pumpkins ready to harvest, to jack-o-lanterns and then to seeds again.
1. Pumpkin Juvenile literature. 2. Pumpkin—Life cycles Juvenile literature. [1. Pumpkin.] I. Thaler, Shmuel, ill. II. Title.
SB347.L48 1999
635'.62—DC21   99-20081
                                                                                    CIP

First printing, 1999. / First paperback printing, 2002.
Printed in China

ISBN-10: 1-58246-004-3 hc
ISBN-13: 978-1-58246-004-8 hc / 9 10 11 12 13 — 10 09 08 07 06
ISBN-10: 1-58246-078-7 ppk
ISBN-13: 978-1-58246-078-9 ppk / 6 7 8 9 — 10 09 80 07 06

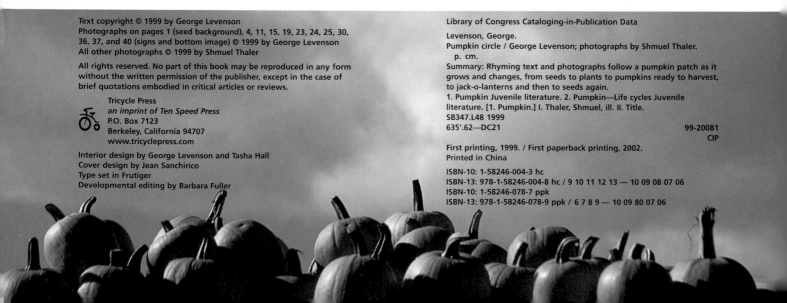